WENDELL PHILLIPS, ESQ.

ON

A METROPOLITAN POLICE.

PHONOGRAPHICALLY REPORTED FOR THE BOSTON TRAVELLER,
BY J. M. W. YERRINTON.

WENDELL PHILLIPS, Esq., spoke at the Melodeon on Sunday, April 5th, 1863, before the Twenty-Eighth Congregational Society, advocating the establishment of a Metropolitan Police. Notwithstanding the dismal weather, the hall was crowded. After the usual preliminary Sunday services, Mr. Phillips said:

I have been requested to speak to you, to-day, on the subject of a Metropolitan Police. That plan has been already presented, two or three years ago, to this community, and, of late, very elaborately and eloquently argued before a Committee of the Legislature, by Edward L. Peirce, Esq., and still more comprehensively and in detail, by Charles M. Ellis, Esq.: but it is one of vital importance to the welfare and progress of our city, and until the object be achieved, it can never be too frequently considered and urged. Other cities have led the way in this path, years ago.

The capital of the civilized world, London, many years ago, found herself utterly unable to contend with the evils of accumulated population—found municipal machinery utterly inadequate for the security of life or property in her streets; and the national government, by the hand of Sir Robert Peel, assumed the police regulation of that cluster of towns which we call London. New York, on our continent, about six years ago, followed the example; Baltimore and Cincinnati have done likewise to a greater or less extent, and so also have some of the other Western cities. The experience of all great accumulations of property and population reads us a lesson, that the execution of the laws therein demand extra consideration and peculiar machinery. Hitherto, the police regulations in the city of Boston have been modelled on those of a small town; that is, the inhabitants themselves have called into existence a body of constables, in fact, to execute the laws of the State and the by-laws of the city. Our text, in presenting this subject to you, is this: in Boston, as everywhere else where large numbers are massed together and great masses of property are found, a police force appointed by the voters of the place cannot be relied on to execute the law; and, in order to secure their full and impartial execution, it has been found necessary elsewhere, and I shall attempt to show you that it is necessary here, to put the control of the police force into other hands than those of the voters of the peninsula. That is our claim—that the men of the peninsula, like those of other great cities, are not to be trusted with the execution of the State laws, but that executive power must be based on broader foundations. Such a course is no uncommon machinery in democratic institutions. We put the interpretation of the laws—the Judiciary—not into the hands of any local municipal body, but the interpretation of the laws is in the hands of persons appointed by the whole State. I invoke the same principle for their execution—following old republican precedents, as I shall shortly show.

In order to sustain this claim before you, I ought to show three or four things. First, that in important particulars—*important* particulars—the law has failed of execution; that good and vitally important laws have failed of execution. Secondly, I ought to show you that this failure is due to the machinery which the city puts in motion for the execution of the laws. Thirdly, that a better machinery may be found. And, fourthly, that it is important for the welfare of the State that the attempt to find a better machinery should be made.

My first point is to show you that in important particulars, where great and grave interests are involved, the laws have failed of execution. You perceive that this involves, in fact, an indictment against the city government. It is in reality arraigning the government of the city for failure to do its duty. Before I pass to it, therefore, let me make one protest. I do not come here to find fault with individual policemen. I think our body of police is as good, on the average, as that of any great city I know. I think upon all trying occasions they have done their duty, as far as they have been permitted, and have always shown full capacity to do their whole duty. Neither do I come here to arraign the individuals of the city government; not, however, on account of the same excuse, but because I deem it unnecessary. They are mere puppets, fluttering before us for a little while; they are only victims of a great system which they did not originate and cannot control. Looking over the last dozen years, considering that the Mayor and Aldermen during those years have been, in the aggregate, only a standing committee appointed by the grog-shops of the peninsula, it has been no honor, but a shame, to hold one of its offices. No man with a full measure of self-respect could accept such an office. All politics necessitates questionable compliances; but this serfdom touches a base depth. But it is not necessary, and certainly not within my purview to-day, to arraign individuals. I am merely criticising a system which throws up, into unfitting places and undue importance, men who have no real right to the power which they are wholly unable or unwilling to use.

To return now to my first point, I am to tell you that, in many important particulars, the laws have failed of execution. I shall take, in the first place, Temperance. Some men look upon this Temperance cause as whining bigotry, narrow asceticism, or a vulgar sentimentality, fit for little minds, weak women and weaker men. On the contrary, I regard it as second only to one or two others of the primary reforms of this age, and for this reason: Every race has its peculiar temptation; every clime has its specific sin. The tropics and tropical races are tempted to one form of sensuality; the colder and temperate regions, and our Saxon blood, find their peculiar temptation in the stimulus of drink and food. In old times, our Heaven was a drunken revel. We relieve ourselves from the over-weariness of constant and exhausting toil by intoxication. Science has brought a cheap means of drunkenness within the reach of every individual; and national prosperity and institutions have put into the hands of almost every workman the means of being drunk for a week on the labor of two or three hours. With that blood and that temptation, we have adopted democratic institutions, where the law has no sanction but the purpose and virtue of the masses. The statute-book rests not on the bayonets of Europe, but on the hearts of the people. A drunken people can never be the basis of a free government. It is the corner-stone neither of virtue, prosperity, nor progress. To us, therefore, the title-deeds of whose estates and the safety of whose lives depend upon the tranquillity of the streets, upon the virtue of the masses, the presence of any vice that brutalizes the average mass of mankind, tends to make it more readily the tool of intriguing and corrupt leaders, is necessarily a stab at the very life of the nation. Against such a vice is marshalled the Temperance Reformation. That my sketch is no mere fancy picture, every one of you know. Every one of you can glance back over your own path, and count many and many a one among those who started from the goal at your side, with equal energy and perhaps greater promise, who has found a drunkard's grave long before this. The brightness of the bar, the ornament of the pulpit, the hope and blessing and stay of many a family—you know, every one of you who has reached middle life, how often on your path you set up the warning—"Fallen before the temptations of the streets!" Hardly one house in this city, whether it be full and warm with all the luxury of wealth, or whether it find hard, cold maintenance by the most earnest economy, no matter which—hardly a house that does not count among sons or nephews, some victim of this vice. The skeleton of this warning sits at every board. The whole world is kindred in this suffering. The country mother launches her boy with trembling upon the temptations of city life; the father trusts his daughter anxiously to the young man she has chosen, knowing what a wreck intoxication may make of the house-tree they set up. Alas! how often are their worst forebodings more than fulfilled! I have known a case—and probably many of you can recall some almost equal to it—where one worthy woman could count father, brother, husband, and son-in-law, all drunkards—no man among her near kindred, except her son, who was not a victim of this vice. Like all other appetites, this finds resolution weak when set against the constant presence of temptation. This is the evil. How are the laws relating to it executed in this city? Let me tell you.

First, there has been great discussion of this evil— wide, earnest, patient discussion, for thirty-five years. The whole community has been stirred by the discussion of this question. Finally, after various experiments, the majority of the State decided that the method to stay this evil was to stop the open sale of intoxicating drink. They left moral suasion still to address the individual, and set themselves as a community to close the doors of temptation. Every man acquainted with his own nature or with society knows that weak virtue, walking through our streets, and meeting at every tenth door (for that is the average) the temptation to drink, must fall; that one must be a moral Hercules to pass unstained. To prevent the open sale of intoxicating liquor has been the method selected by the State to help its citizens to be virtuous; in other words, the State has enacted what is called the Maine Liquor Law. You may drink in your own parlors, you may make what indulgence you please your daily rule, the State does not touch you there; there you injure only yourself, and those you directly influence; that the State cannot reach. But when you open your door and say to your fellow-citizens, "Come and indulge," the State has a right to ask, "In what do you invite them to indulge? Is it in something that helps, or something that harms, the community?"

I will try to show you, in a moment, on what

grounds the State decided that these numberless open doors harmed the community, and that the method to be adopted was to shut them up. The majority, after full argument in district school-houses, the streets and the State-house, from pulpits, lyceum platforms, and everywhere else, decided that prohibition of the traffic was the only effective method. The law was put upon the statute-book. A reluctant minority went to the Legislature, and endeavored to repeal or amend it, alleging that this was not a good law; and they were voted down. Again they went—were voted down. A third time they went—and were voted down. They then appealed to the Courts, and said, "This is not a constitutional law." The Courts said, "It is." If anything ever had the decided, unmistakable sanction of a majority of the people of this Commonwealth, the Maine Liquor Law has it. After a quarter of a century of discussion, it was enacted; three times assailed, it was maintained; subjected to the crucible of the Court, it came out pure gold. We have a right to say that it is the matured, settled purpose of the majority of the Commonmealth; if the majority have a right to govern, that law is to govern. Have we not? If not, let the minority assail again the Gibraltar of the statute. But meanwhile it is, like all other laws not immoral, to be obeyed. I have not, therefore, to argue to-day whether the law is good or not, whether it is wise or not. That is settled. It is good and wise in the opinion of the Commonwealth. The era of *public opinion* is finished, that of *law* has commenced. This is the history of all legislation. Do not find fault with us for enacting, in due time, public opinion into a statute. Where did all statutes come from? Hundreds of years ago, men argued the question, "Shall one man own a separate piece of land?" They argued it, and settled that he should. That became a statute. They then began to argue the question, "Shall he transmit to his children by will?" They argued that for centuries, then said, "Yes," and enacted it. Nobody now goes behind those statutes. Hundreds of years ago, our race argued the question, "Shall a man have one wife, or three?" We settled that he should have but one; it is the law of the Commonwealth.

The era of discussion and opinion is over; the era of legislation has come; the time when the minority sits down and obeys. With all great questions, covering important interests, there is a time when public opinion stereotypes itself into statutes. Land, wheat, marriage, the rules against burglary and theft, settled themselves years ago. If I raise a harvest, it is mine; that is the law of the land. There was a time when it was a question; it is not a question now. So with temperance and the Maine liquor law. Time was when the question whether a man had a right to sell liquor openly, unlicensed, was discussed; we have passed that point, and reached the time when the majority, in other words, the State, decrees that these shops shall be shut.

Now, let me show you, in a few words, *why* it should

decree that. Let me show it by an instance. Take our city. Our city met that statute thus:—It said, "You may decree it if you please, we won't execute it. You say we shall not license anybody, but we will effect the same thing, for we will let everybody sell, except just those whom we should not have licensed." These are the exact words of the order to the police some years ago. The Chief of Police replied to a question from the Massachusetts Temperance Society, "We have directions never to prosecute a liquor seller, unless he be one who would not have received a license under the old license act." In other words, the State says, "On mature consideration, I prohibit the sale." The city says, "I shall allow it—help yourself!" Those whom it would not have licensed are "nuisances," as it calls them, houses vulgar, noisy, disorderly; kept, as the Dogberry of the Board of Aldermen told us at the State House, by "imbecile old men and ancient women"—as the constable of Shakspeare's play arrested all "vagrom men." That is the position of the city. The law is intentionally and avowedly set aside. The City Government announces that it does not intend to obey it; makes no effort and never has to enforce it. What is the result? The result is that there are at least 3000 places in the city where liquor is publicly and continually sold. These consist partly of dram shops, partly of gambling saloons, partly of houses of prostitution. They number in all more than 3000; I am giving an under estimate of an average for two or three years. What are the results of these 3000 places of sale? Six million dollars' worth of liquor is sold to the retailers of this city annually; and three million dollars' worth is annually retailed on the peninsula. With what result? With this. They produce poverty and crime to this extent:—We arrest for drunkenness alone, on an average for the last three years, about 17,000 persons annually; that is, a little less than one-tenth of the population. There are between twenty-five and thirty thousand persons relieved for poverty by overseers of the poor, and by the Provident Association—poverty caused by intemperance. That is, every seventh man in the city is a pauper, helped by the community; every tenth man in the city is a criminal, arrested by the police. Let us look at that a moment. I say every seventh man is a pauper, relieved by the help of the community. Poverty, wholesome poverty, is no unmixed evil; it is the motive power that throws a man up to guide and control the community; it is the spur that often wins the race; it is the trial that calls out, like fire, all the deep, great qualities of a man's nature. That poverty is no evil—at least, it is no unmixed evil; but poverty that is caused by drunkenness—for I am only taking, in these 25,000 persons, the poverty that is traceable to intemperance—the poverty that is caused by drunkenness has what history? The father is a drunkard; the mother often imitates him; the self-respect of the family is lost; the home is gone; it is a scene of quarrel and degradation; the children are thrown neglected on the streets, with no food, no education, no moral sense developed,—the frightful and fruitful source of every vice known to the civil code. That feeds the gallows, fills the street with impurity, makes thieves and burglars. Out of these houses flows a constant supply for all forms of crime. Without the open and continued sale of drink, almost every hell of the gambler would be closed; he would have few victims. He would find few men in the mood to be victimized. Without open places for the sale of liquor, the houses of prostitution could not be maintained; that is the testimony of all experience in every city. To that shameless pit woman seldom sinks, except when betrayed by drink—and even when once ruined, could not bear such a life unless nature was daily stupified by intoxication. Nine-tenths of those sent to the House of Industry are common drunkards. Intemperance is the most productive of all causes of insanity. "Truancy" finds its "cause of causes" in intemperance. Said the Chief of Police, three or four years ago, "Intemperance is the direct origin of more poverty, more crime, and consequent suffering, than all other causes combined." Twenty-five thousand men reduced to poverty in a year, or at least every year relieved by the public.

Now let me go to the schools. Twenty-five thousand is an average estimate of the children who attend our public schools. The city pours out a quarter of a million a year to mould those young souls, step by step, to virtue, to make them good citizens. Twenty-five thousand with one hand it lifts up; with the other it forces down twenty-five thousand into pollution and crime. It spends $477,000 a year to do it; for that is the cost of our police force, of cur overseers of the poor, of our lunatic asylums, (a large portion of whose inmates are rendered insane by intemperance,) our house of correction and house of industry. You might as well take a third of a million of dollars, and toss it off the end of long wharf—we should be richer at the end of the year. Leave all the children idle in the streets, shut up the grog-shops, shut up the schools, throw a third of a million into the water, and the city would be better off on the 31st day of December than she is now.

That is the cost of intemperance. One-half the criminals of the State are found in the city of Boston. We have one-sixth of the population, and yet we have more than one half the criminals. We have one-sixth of the population, but we pay about one-half of the criminal expenses of the State of Massachusetts—just three times our proper proportion. What does it come from? I am not to charge it on any particular corporation; I am to charge it to a system. It is the massing up of one-third of the capital of the State, and one-sixth the population on this peninsula. That makes a new order of things, one calling for a new machinery to check crime; a hot-bed, where all the tendencies to crime become doubled and trebled, where the dangerous classes of the community get undue power. It is because of that peculiarity, that we need a different system from what the country does. Up to a certain point, our city government has always acknowledged this. For instance, in a small country town of a few thousand inhabitants they have two or three constables. Nobody knows who they are. You might visit half a dozen houses, and they could not not tell you. Only once or twice in a year, on some festive or other occasion, a town meeting, a picnic, or something of the kind, is he ever seen or needed. He may execute a writ once in a while. If there is any disorder in the town, a citizen takes notice of it, reports it to a justice of the peace, and the difficulty is cured. That is a sufficient machinery for a small town. But, when you have a large and dense population, great wealth invested in certain dangerous and tempting forms, you cannot trust the execution of the laws to the volunteer efforts of the citizens ; you must have a large body of police, constantly in the streets, ever on the alert, with grave powers, with extraordinary functions, to watch criminals and follow them up. That has been found necessary. Now, the question is whether something further is not necessary also. The returns for ten years show that 42 per cent. of the average population of this county was arrested for crime, while, in other counties, the number arrested was only one, two or three per cent. Why this difference ? Because a city necessarily induces greater temptations, greater dangers, and more frequent crimes. It needs, therefore, a more stringent machinery to execute the laws. Instead of that, in regard to this temperance law, the city government defy it. They, themselves, pay—or did pay till within a year or two, I will not speak of the present year, for I have not consulted the reports—about a thousand dollars a month out of the city treasury for the indulgences of the Board of Aldermen and Common Councilmen at an illegal liquor shop, which no one of them had a right to see without presenting it to the courts within twenty-four hours. In that disgraceful Anthony Burns and Sims experience of the city, upon which I am shortly to speak, one of the melancholy features of city sin that day was, that the men illegally called out to defy the State laws contracted a bill, within sight of the Supreme Court, within sight of City Hall, of between one and two thousand dollars, for liquor and food furnished them at an illegal grogshop, by order of the city.

Let me pause a moment on this question, and turn to another—Free Speech. Free Speech is so vital an element of civil life, so important a privilege, that the framers of our government were not willing to leave it to the law—they enshrined it in the Constitution. It was so fundamental that it could not be left to annual legislation; it was grouted and dovetailed into the very first stratum of the foundation of the State. Now, the class of men who have had the ordering of city affairs have never, for the last twenty years, attempted to protect free speech on this peninsula. Let me tell you what I mean. If a man like the editor of the Boston *Post,* like the Hon. Edward Everett, like Mr. Sumner, any popular person in the community, wished to hold a meeting on this peninsula, he could always do it; but if any set of men who are unpopular wanted to hold a meeting here, it depended entirely upon the mood of the mob that month whether they could hold it or not. These very walls could testify, if they had voice, how many dozen times they have seen their occupants, paying an honest price for a day's use of them, disturbed hour after hour, and finally, perhaps, in some instances, the meeting broken up, by a crowd of boys that the right hand of one policeman could have quelled; and when individuals, the very lessees of this hall, would take one of these disturbers to the courts, he was set free, and the persons who interfered threatened with a suit. You know that the trustees of the hall from which you have just removed for a season, sat on one occasion until midnight, to decide whether they would dare to risk their property when the Mayor of the city had let it be known that he did not intend to defend it against the mob of the streets. You know too, or you might know, that the same anxious scene of consultation went on among the trustees of the Tremont Temple, again and again, whether they would dare to risk their building, when the city authorities had unblushingly and publicly declared that they would not protect free speech. You know, also, that the State herself did not venture to grant the use of the State House to a body of men turned out by the Mayor of the city from their own hall, when the members of the Legislature expressed their willingness to do it, because the Executive informed them that he had no means to protect the State's property against the grog-shops of the peninsula. Macaulay says, speaking of James the Second's disturbed reign: "On such occasions, it will ever be found that the human vermin, which, neglected by ministers of State and ministers of religion—barbarians in the midst of civilization, heathen in the midst of Christianity—who burrow among all physical and moral pollution in the cellars and garrets of great cities, will rise at once into terrible importance." It was when that class of the community found that the Mayor was willing to lead them, and that they could riot in the most gilded drinking saloons free of expense, that your Governor dared not trust the State House to an orderly and legal assemblage of the citizens of Massachusetts. It was at a time when one of the most efficient of the Chiefs of Police said, "Give me thirty men, *and an order*, and I will quell that mob at once." The difficulty was not that it could not be quelled. That class which Macaulay describes never faces the law until it has bribed it. The moment the Court turns its determined countenance upon them, they retire to cellars and garrets again. One of the Aldermen of the city said recently, in the State House, that these mobs were only "watermelon frolics—the pounding of men with the soft side of a cushion;" but it was a cushion that the Governor dared not trust to touch the State House; it was a mob which the Mayor said, in excuse for inefficiency, that he had not force enough to control. Perhaps it would not be disrespectful to ask that these several city dignitaries would arrange beforehand, and make their lame excuses at least consistent. There is a class of whom an old proverb affirms that it needs to have "long memories."

Fellow-citizens, for the last five years, I have been able to make, in New York, in perfect quiet, with the unsolicited protection of the police, the same speech which I could not make to you without being surrounded by fifty armed friends. Again and again have I proved this, during the last five years. In the city of New York, the common sewer of the continent, where wealth is massed up by uncounted millions, where the criminals of all nations take refuge, any man could speak his mind for the last five years; and if the journals threatened him with violence, he need not go begging to the City Hall—as we vainly used to do here: the authorities would take notice, unsolicited, and see to it that he was protected. But, at the same time, in our own city, of one-quarter part of the inhabitants, it was impossible, without personal protection, to utter the same words. Why is this? It is no fault of individuals, as I said before. Three thousand places where drink is sold! Do I exaggerate when I say that each one of those places represents a voter? Mr. Ellis has said, with great force, that every one of those places represents at least ten men whom it influences, which would make thirty thousand—and doubtless his estimate understates the fact; but I am not going to speak of those whom those places influence. I am going to speak of the voters which they send to the polls, and I certainly shall not exaggerate if I say, that each one of them influences one voter—the owner of the shop, the keeper, the tender, or the frequenter of it. There are 3000 voters—certainly I should not exaggerate if I said 5000. About 15,000 voters on this peninsula usually go to the polls, sometimes 22,000, though very rarely. Now, 3000 voters could always hold the balance in such a constituency—Republican, Democratic, Catholic, Protestant. With all varieties of opinion and purpose, three thousand men, bound together by one idea, one interest, with one purpose in view, and demanding one thing, and nothing more, can always hold the balance. There never was a city election which that number of votes massed together could not control. What is the result? The result is, that it is as much a bargain as if it were recorded in the Registry of Deeds, that the prominent aspirants for city office shall not execute the laws against the liquor shops. Is it at all remarkable? A great many men want office—it is an American failing. Here are the men who can bestow it. They say—"This is the condition: shut your eyes upon us!" The consequence is, that both parties, all parties, are obliged to bow their necks to that yoke, and, with rare exceptions, there cannot be an Alderman nor a Mayor of the city elected, who is not understood to be willing to shut his eyes to that crime, and leave the law of the State unexecuted. It has been so, it always must be so, while these elements of civic strength exist, and are thus tempted to exert themselves.

The reason why the law is not executed in favor of free speech is germane and sister to this; it is, that the men who are interested in these drinking shops, and the men whose votes they can command, are of the class that hates progress and freedom—is naturally antagonistic to them; and any designing leader can stir up such a mass, and fling it at virtue, and order, and liberty. Hence these consequences. Their agents, of their own natural bias, run greedily to do such agreeable work.

For the last ten or thirteen years, this has been the machinery of the city government. They have said to the State, "We will not execute your law." Now, law consists of four things—a statute, a policeman to arrest the offender, a jury to try him, and a judge to sentence him. The Constitution says, we shall have judges "as impartial as the lot of humanity admits." We have them. Chosen, how? By the State. The other end of the telegraph is a man to bring the offender before the judge. What is the use of a judge? He cannot move of himself; he is powerless if you do not bring the criminals before him. But the city government of Boston, chosen by this machinery I have spoken of, says to its police officers, "Don't you furnish that judge with any criminals; shut your eyes upon them!" Then, again, if one is arrested, by any accident, what more? Why, this: the statute says that our jurymen shall be drawn from a box, in which the names of citizens of good moral character and sound judgment, free from all legal exceptions, are put. The city weeds out the jury-box on another plan. In all trials that had anti-slavery or temperance in them, you might be certain of one thing—you would never see an abolitionist nor a temperance man on the jury. If he got there, it was an accident, and there was always enough to neutralize it. It is just like the black element. We have several thousand black men in our community; you have never seen a black man on a jury but once, and that was an accident, and he was not allowed to sit, though he had been regularly drawn. Many of them are of good moral character, but their names never get into the box; or, if they get in, never come out. So of a man known, distinctively, as an abolitionist; if his name goes in, it never comes out. So of a man known as a temperance man; rarely does his name come out. But liquor dealers have always been abundant; no jury was trusted alone without them. If the State furnishes good judges, and the city, at the other end, furnishes no criminals, or, when one is by chance caught, fortifies him with a jury that will disagree on his side, how is the law to be executed? As long as the city government is chosen by men whose interest is on that side, how can it be otherwise? How is the law to be executed, when you have entrusted its execution to men who do not wish or mean to execute it; who were elected expressly not to execute it, and have the strongest motive not to do so? No matter how good individual policemen are, while such men rule them. You know when Baillie Nicol Jarvie, in Scott's immortal novel, let Rob Roy out of jail—he was an Alderman, a Baillie, and let him out—he said to Rob, "If you continue to be such a thief, you ought to have a doorkeeper in every jail in Scotland.' "O, no, Baillie," replied Rob, "it is just as well to have a *Baillie* in every borough." It answers the same purpose to have a servile and complacent Mayor and Aldermen as to have fettered policemen, because they settle the juries, and they settle the functions of the police. The consequence has been, that there has been no effort to execute the law. The defence put in is, "We cannot execute the law." The Mayor said of the riots of 1860–'61, "We can't put them down." The reply of his own policemen was, "Thirty of us will put them down, if you will allow us." The reply of the Abolitionist was, "When did you ever make an effort to put them down? The only time you ever stood on Tremont Temple platform and issued an order, it was obeyed; the mob recognized you as their leader." But men say at the State House, in reply to the eloquent argument of Mr. Ellis—Mr. Healy, Alderman Amory said—"We cannot execute an unpopular law." Indeed! Indeed! I can remember when Marshal Tukey put a chain round your Court House to execute a law that was hated by the Commonwealth of Massachusetts full as bitterly as Beacon street hates the Maine Liquor Law; and I can remember when he went up to a legislative committee appointed to examine into his conduct, and inquire why a policeman of the city of Boston was acting in that illegal manner, against the statute of the State, and answered Mr. Keyes, "Sir, I know it is illegal, but I mean to do it. Help yourself!"

In 1843, Latimer was arrested by a policeman with a lie in his mouth. In 1851, Sims was surrendered by policemen acting illegally, and avowing their defiance. In 1854, Burns was sent back, and his claimants were aided by the police, contrary to the statute. Unpopular laws! The city can execute anything it wants to, unpopular or popular. The city executes every one of its own by-laws perfectly. No man steals with impunity; no man violates Sunday with impunity; no man sets up a nuisance with impunity. As the Grand Jury said, several years ago, "The municipal authorities can remove this nuisance, or at least abate it, whenever they will. It is as much in their power as the offal in the sewers or the dirt in the streets."

Tell 180,000 Yankees that they cannot execute a law when they wish to! Once, by happy accident, our Mayor left the city, and an exceptional but most unexceptionable Alderman, Mr. Otis Clapp, took his place—no trouble that day in quelling the mob. Deputy Chief Ham did it in thirty minutes. It is only the presence of Mayors that makes mobs omnipotent. But suppose Mayors cannot execute the laws—what then? If Berkshire should say, "We want, every one of us, to have two wives," and practise it, and send word up to Boston, "We cannot execute the other law," do you think we should sit down quietly, and let it go? How long?

Boston has five or six trains of railroads—one to the Old Colony, one to Providence, one to Worcester, one to Lowell, one to Fitchburg, one to the eastern counties. All of them run locomotives where they wish to. Suppose that, on the Fitchburg railroad, one locomotive, for a year, never got further than Groton—what do you think the Directors of the road would do? Would they take up the rails beyond Groton, or would they turn out the engineer? There is a law of the Commonwealth of Massachusetts, thoroughly executed in every county but ours; and here the men appointed to execute it not only do not want to, but you cannot expect them to. They were elected *not* to execute it, and they say they can't execute it. Shall we take up the rails, or change the engineer?—which?

Men say, to take the appointment of the police out of the hands of the peninsula is anti-democratic. Why, from 1620 down to within ten years, the State always acted on that plan. The State makes the law. Who executes it? The State. For two hundred years, the Governor appointed the Sheriff of every county, and the Sheriff appointed his deputies, and they executed the laws. The constables of the towns were allowed merely subsidiary authority to execute by-laws, and help execute the State law. The democratic principle is, that the law shall be executed by an executive authority concurrent with that which makes it. That is democracy. The State law, naturally, democratically, is to be executed by the State. We have merely, in deference to convenience, changed that of late in some particulars, and we may reasonably go back to it if we find that, in any particular locality, the new plan fails. Why not? In all other matters of State concern, as Mr. Ellis has well shown,—Board of Education, Board of Agriculture, and all the various Boards,—the State has the control. You perceive this "anti-democratic" argument can be carried out to an absurdity. Suppose the Five Points of New York should send word to the Fifth Avenue—"We don't like your police; we mean to have one of our own, and it will be very anti-democratic for you to take the choice of our own constables out of our own hands." Suppose North street should send word to City Hall—"We have concluded to turn every other house into a grog-shop, or something almost as bad, and to appoint our own police; please instruct your police to keep out of our ward." We should not say this was democratic. We should say, that as far as the interest of a community in a law extends, just so far that community has a right to a hand in the execution of it. Now, the State of Massachusetts feels an interest in the execution of the Maine Liquor Law. We have a sixth of the population and a third of the wealth of the State. Do the influences of these stop with the people who sleep on this peninsula? Does not our influence radiate in every direction? Do not twenty thousand men do business here who do not sleep here ? A third of the wealth ! Who owns it ? We that sleep here ? Not at all. These costly railroad depots, these rich banks, these large aggregates of property, who own them ? Why, the men that live ten, twenty, thirty miles outside of the city limits, and come in here in crowds the first of January, April, July and October, to get there dividends. Men who have millions invested on this peninsula no interest in knowing whether the streets are safe ! Sending their sons into our streets—no interest in their being morally wholesome ! Trusting their lives here—no interest in their being safe !

A fortnight ago, a woman, a teacher in a country town within twenty miles of Boston, missed her father —an honest, temperate farmer, though not a teetotaller. He came to the city to sell cattle, and had received five hundred dollars. He had been gone a week, and she came down to the city to hunt him up. She traced him from spot to spot, and finally found that the grog-shops had gotten hold of him, made him drunk, taken his money, kept him drunk three days, so that a convenient policeman might see him that number of times and complain of him as a common drunkard, and he had gone to the House of Correction for three months. Has that town no interest in the streets of Boston ? Let me tell you again a story that I have told you once or twice before, for it holds a deep moral. A few years ago, one spring afternoon, when I left the city to deliver a lecture, I alighted from the railroad car at the foot of a hill, whose swelling side was crowned with the most magnificent of country dwellings. Architecture and Horticulture had exhausted their art. It was so unlike any thing about it, I was led to ask how it came there. The man who was driving me said it was built by a village boy, who wanted to show how much money he had made in Boston in fifteen years. "He left here without a cent," said the young man—"went to Boston—became a distiller—returned with two hundred thousand dollars—that is his residence." Do you suppose there was a Yankee boy within sight of that hill-side who was not tempted to repeat that Boston experience, of rapid and easy wealth? I rode on fourteen miles, and was set down opposite one of those village homes which Dr. Holmes describes—a square house of the Revolutionary period—old elms hung over the lawn before it. The same driver said, "In that front room lies dying the grandson of the man who built that house. Grandfather and father died drunkards—lay about the streets of the village drunk. That boy and I started together in life. He went with me to Lowell. We went through the mills and a mechanic trade. Never did one drop of intoxicating liquor pass his lips. Social frolic, increase of means, friendly entreaty, gay hours never tempted him. Until thirty, he stood untouched, guarded by an iron resolution. Having gathered a few thousands, he was tempted to Boston for a wider trade. He went there—stayed six years; came home penniless and a drunkard, to lie in the very streets where his father and grandfather had lain before. He could stand up against every temptation, except Boston streets. There he lies dying, as his grandfather and father before him." Do you say that the people of these country towns have no interest in the streets of Boston? You tempt the virtue, melt the resolution and corrupt the morals of the Commonwealth, as far as your influence extends.

No interest! Let me go a little ways off, and be less invidious. New York has one-fifth of the population of the State on Manhattan Island. Recently, in a great national convulsion, the city stirred herself to checkmate the State. For Wadsworth, the candidate of order, of liberty, of government, the country counties flung twenty thousand majority. The demons of discord stirred up the purlieus of the city, and flung thirty thousand against him. Ten thousand, the ultimate majority, carried their candidate to Albany. What was his first blow? Seymour's first act, when he assumed the Governorship, what was it? He fulfilled his bargain. He hurled his defiance at the Metropolitan Police that kept him and his allies, conspirators, from carrying the Empire State into the hands of the Confederacy. Those are the times, when, as Macaulay says, "the vermin burrowing in garrets and cellars show themselves of terrible importance." Who knows that such times may not come upon us?

I have seen the day, in that city of New York, when Rynders dictated law to the Chief of Police, and Matsell obeyed him. For twenty years, I have seen, in your city, the mob rule when they pleased. I have seen your Mayor order his police, in Faneuil Hall, to take off their badges and join the mob that crowded out free speech from that consecrated hall. You saw, two years ago, the State government reeling before the victims of the Tremont House and Parker House. The Governor complained then, as I am told he does now, that in the whole county, he had not one single officer whom he could command to execute the law. Who shall say that the security of this great centre of wealth and population is not for the interest, for the peace, for the absolute prosperity of the State? We, too, may have a Fernando Wood—who knows? Our sixth part of the population of the State may attempt, in the interest of liquor and despotism, to defy the Commonwealth. It is too important a machinery to be left in the hands of the dangerous classes. We want to take it out of the hands of the dangerous classes, and put it into the hands of the Commonwealth—nothing else. One of two things is necessary. The law is bad—repeal it; or the law is good—keep it. No other county would be allowed to defy the law—why this?

The Mayor says he cannot execute it. Take him at his word. Undoubtedly, HE cannot, for he was chosen not to; but the question is, can it be executed? What do the temperance majority of the Commonwealth claim? One trial—nothing more. We have funded twenty-five years of discussion, any amount of toil and labor, in that statute. It never has had one trial yet on this peninsula. May we not ask simply one trial? The locomotive has never *attempted* to go beyond Groton. Why take up the rails yet? If Berkshire should say, "We can't execute your law against polygamy," what should we do? Why, appoint fresh sheriffs, not repeal the law. So in this case, let not Massachusetts get down and say, "I, too, am a slave to the grog-shops of the peninsula."

We do not claim that drunkenness can be wholly rooted out. But we do claim that this law can be executed as perfectly as other laws are, if its execution be entrusted to competent and faithful hands. No crime is wholly prevented. Our crowded prisons prove that. No law is perfectly executed. But there is nothing in the Maine Liquor Law that distinguishes it from other statutes. No man claims that the *use* of intoxicating drink can be wholly stopped. But it is idle and ridiculous to say that the *public sale* of it cannot be stopped as much as the indiscriminate keeping of gunpowder, or the opening of shops on Sunday, or the firing of muskets in crowded streets, whenever magistrates shall really wish and mean to do their duty.

A metropolitan police has been necessary in London, and now its streets are the safest in the world. In New York it has saved the city from convulsion and bloodshed. One of its prominent citizens said to me, a short time ago, "You do not know how near we have been to an outbreak in this very street. But for our police, the attempt would have been made to surrender us to Southern dictation." That same civil disorder may impend over us. What is the remedy? Let the State hold her hand on the vices of the peninsula—claim her old democratic right to execute the laws she has made—to execute them if the city cannot, or if, by her constitution of government, she will not try to execute them faithfully.

Our plan is to have Commissioners—three or five—appointed by the Governor or by the Legislature, whichever seems best. Let them hold their offices for three or five years; they appoint, rule, and remove the members of the police force. Such a Commission would be removed, as far as anything in our civil system is or ought to be, from the control of party politics, and would be largely independent of the "dangerous classes." This peninsula needs it immediately—the neighboring towns and cities will need it soon. The members of such a police force should hold their places during good behavior, and be removed only on charges stated in writing, to which they may have a chance of replying. Now, every fall, the liquor dealer or other criminal, whom an honest policeman has troubled, holds up his warning finger to the Alderman of that Ward—"Remove that policeman, or don't expect my vote." What officer can be expected to do his duty in such circumstances?

The moment the liquor interest of the city see that their mixing in city elections will not secure a police force in their interest, they will probably leave the election of Mayor and Aldermen to the natural action of ordinary politics, and then we shall have as good officers as our system will secure, with the present level of education. Such Mayors and Aldermen will, probably, no longer prostitute the jury box to defend rum and shield mobs. They will have no interest to do so. But if they do, we must press forward, and find a remedy for that. I have full faith in democratic institutions. Work on, and we shall yet lift them up to much higher perfection. The future is sure. Honest men rule in the end. Only show them their interest and duty, and, in due time, they will rally to do it. Ten years ago, I made an anti-slavery speech, painting Southern despotism, and demanding that the North should rouse herself against her tyrants. The next day, meeting the oldest statesman of the Commonwealth, he said to me, "Your speech was all true. I knew it thirty years ago. But what can you do about it? They wont listen." I answered, "I mean to protest—claim my rights, and denounce those who assail them, whether they listen or not." The policy has been somewhat successful. Agitate! and we shall yet see the laws of Massachusetts rule even Boston.

www.ingramcontent.com/pod-product-compliance
Lightning Source LLC
LaVergne TN
LVHW020742120826
845150LV00010B/2344